# OTTERS

*by Katie Marsico*

**Children's Press®**

An Imprint of Scholastic Inc.

New York   Toronto   London   Auckland   Sydney
Mexico City   New Delhi   Hong Kong
Danbury, Connecticut

Content Consultant
Dr. Stephen S. Ditchkoff
Professor of Wildlife Sciences
Auburn University
Auburn, Alabama

Photographs ©: Alamy Images: 4, 5, 28, 29 (Cathy Hart
Photography/Alaska Stock), 20, 21 (Darren Olley), 5 top, 12 (Glenn
Bartley/All Canada Photos), 30, 31 (Laura Romin & Larry Dalton),
36, 37 (Max Allen), 14, 15 (Steve Bray), 8, 9, 32 (Tom Stack);
AP Images/Russ Houston: 5 bottom, 40, 41; Dreamstime: 1, 46
(Isselee), 2 (Remigiusz Oprzadek), 3 background, 44 background,
45 background (Remigiusz Oprzadek); Media Bakery: cover (David
Fleetham), 6, 7 (Frans Lanting); Science Source/Thomas & Pat Leeson:
22, 23; Shutterstock, Inc./martyn bennett: 35; Superstock, Inc.: 11
(age fotostock), 26, 27 (Biosphoto), 16 (Ingo Arndt/Minden Pictures),
39 (NHPA); Thinkstock: 24, 25 (Glenn Nagel), 18, 19 (kwiktor).

Map by Bob Italiano

Library of Congress Cataloging-in-Publication Data
Marsico, Katie, 1980– author.
  Otters / by Katie Marsico.
      pages cm. — (Nature's children)
  Summary: "This book details the life and habits of otters."—
Provided by publisher.
  Audience: Ages 9–12.
  Audience: Grades 4 to 6.
  ISBN 978-0-531-21171-7 (library binding) —
  ISBN 978-0-531-21190-8 (pbk.)
  1. Otters—Juvenile literature. I. Title. II. Series: Nature's children
(New York, N.Y.)
  QL737.C25M37 2015
  599.769—dc23
                          2014029891

All rights reserved. Published in 2015 by Children's Press, an imprint
of Scholastic Inc.

Printed in China 62
SCHOLASTIC, CHILDREN'S PRESS, and associated logos are
trademarks and/or registered trademarks of Scholastic Inc.

1 2 3 4 5 6 7 8 9 10 R 24 23 22 21 20 19 18 17 16 15

# Otters

| | |
|---|---|
| **Class** | Mammalia |
| **Order** | Carnivora |
| **Family, Subfamily** | Mustelidae, Lutrinae |
| **Genera** | 7 genera |
| **Species** | 13 species |
| **World distribution** | Found in most parts of the world, excluding Antarctica and Australia |
| **Habitats** | Aquatic areas, including rivers, lakes, streams, marshes, and coastal areas |
| **Distinctive physical characteristics** | Dense, waterproof coat that consists of two layers; four short, powerful legs; webbed toes; muscular tail; streamlined, cylindrical body; thick neck and a flattened head; small ears and eyes located toward the front of the skull |
| **Habits** | Aquatic or semiaquatic; extremely playful; able to create simple tools to eat prey; often use dens of other animals; may build dens; sometimes live in groups; produce one to two litters per year; do not typically mate for life |
| **Diet** | Fish, crayfish, crabs, snails, frogs, sea urchins, clams, mussels, small birds, and rodents |

# Contents

# CHAPTER 1

# Floating in the Kelp Forest

From a distance, the kelp forest along Alaska's coastline appears to be a tangle of green and brown clumps. Up close, it's clear that the water's brown clumps aren't clumps at all—they're sea otters! These aquatic animals are lying on their backs in the mid-morning sunshine. Some members of the group carry a baby on their chest.

As the sea otters gently bob with the rhythm of the waves, there's little chance they'll drift away. By wrapping themselves in kelp leaves, they create a natural anchor that keeps them in place. They are able to eat, sleep, and play while floating.

Sea otters are one of 13 otter species. These carnivorous mammals are either aquatic or semiaquatic. They are also extremely playful and skilled. Some even know how to create simple tools that they use to capture prey!

*A group of sea otters floats among the kelp.*

# Never Far From Water

Otters are found almost everywhere except for Antarctica and Australia. They always live close to a body of water. However, the amount of time they spend in it varies from species to species. For example, river otters usually prefer to be on land unless they're traveling or searching for food. Other species such as sea otters are almost constantly in the water.

Rivers, lakes, streams, marshes, and coastal areas all serve as otter **habitats**. Depending on the species, otters swim in both freshwater and saltwater **environments**. They generally stay within a **home range** of up to 10 square miles (26 square kilometers).

With the exception of sea otters, most species build **dens**—which are called holts or couches—near the water. In many cases, they construct these homes by digging underground or shaping branches and twigs into a nest.

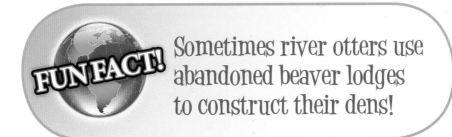

**FUN FACT!** Sometimes river otters use abandoned beaver lodges to construct their dens!

*Dens help otters hide from predators.*

# An Overview of Appearance

Different otter species have different physical characteristics and body sizes. The giant otter is the longest species. It measures up to 7.8 feet (2.4 meters) long. Meanwhile, the Asian small-clawed otter is both the shortest and lightest species. It only reaches a length of 3 feet (0.9 m) and generally weighs no more than 11 pounds (5 kilograms). At 95 pounds (43 kg), the sea otter is nearly nine times as heavy.

Despite some qualities that vary from species to species, all otters share certain physical features. These include a flattened head with a whiskered muzzle, small ears, and eyes located toward the front of the skull. In addition, otters have a long body, a thick neck, four short legs, and a tail. People often compare the texture of the otter's dense fur to velvet. An otter's hair is usually a shade of brown. It is lighter on the animal's underside than its backside.

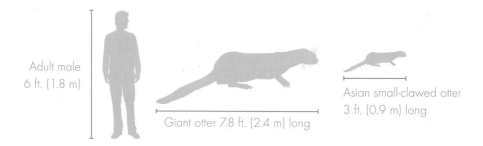

Adult male
6 ft. (1.8 m)

Giant otter 7.8 ft. (2.4 m) long

Asian small-clawed otter
3 ft. (0.9 m) long

*Asian small-clawed otters are found in northern India and across Southeast Asia.*

# CHAPTER 2

# Survival Skills

Thanks to many remarkable adaptations, otters have survived on Earth for millions of years. Traits ranging from waterproof fur to powerful feet help them hunt food and escape danger. Otters' impressive intelligence is another valuable adaptation. Their natural predators include coyotes, bobcats, eagles, alligators, crocodiles, sea lions, sharks, and killer whales.

Depending on the species, otters feed on fish, crayfish, crabs, snails, frogs, sea urchins, clams, and mussels. Some have even been known to hunt small birds and rodents.

Otters need to feed often and in large amounts. Certain species eat up to 30 percent of their own body weight every day. A steady supply of food is necessary to support their fast metabolism. A high metabolic rate provides otters with energy and body heat. This is especially important, because they frequently swim in cold water.

*Fish make up a large part of many otters' diets.*

# A Warm, Waterproof Coat

Unlike seals and whales, otters lack blubber. This layer of body fat is found on many aquatic and semiaquatic mammals. It insulates them against the cold. Because otters don't have blubber, they rely on their extremely dense coat to keep warm.

Some otter species have thicker fur than any other mammal on Earth. Scientists have determined that sea otters have 850,000 to 1 million hairs per every square inch of skin. By comparison, most humans have around 100,000 hairs on their entire head.

An otter's coat is made up of two layers—an undercoat and a topcoat. The undercoat is so dense that it traps heat close to the animal's skin. Meanwhile, the topcoat is made up of long, rough hairs. These hairs form something similar to a waterproof jacket. Many mammals often shed their undercoat in warmer weather, but otters do not. Since water temperature tends to change less than air temperature, otters depend on year-round insulation.

*An otter's dense fur allows it to tolerate chilly aquatic habitats.*

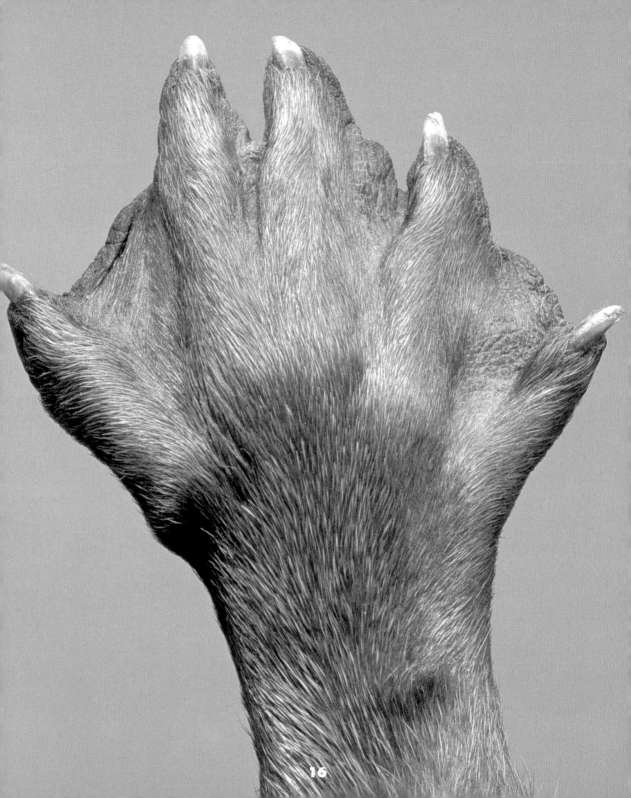

# Paws and Claws

An otter's coat doesn't insulate so well when it is dirty. As a result, otters spend a lot of time grooming. One way they do this is by combing their fur with their paws and claws.

Otters depend on their paws to carry out many other day-to-day activities as well. For example, their webbed toes make it easier to jet forward while swimming. In addition, having five toes on each foot helps otters to stay balanced on land. This is an important skill for animals that regularly climb into and out of water.

With a few exceptions, most otter species have sharp claws. This stops them from slipping and sliding on wet rocks. For species that lack claws, adaptations such as rough skin and flexible front paws serve a similar purpose. Sometimes otters use their claws and paws to hunt prey.

**FUN FACT!** Sea otters spend roughly four to six hours a day grooming.

*For certain species of otter, webbed feet function almost like flippers in the water.*

# Superior Swimmers

An otter's streamlined body is the perfect shape for making smooth, speedy movements through the water. This feature helps some species dive as deep as 300 feet (91 m) in search of food. An otter's strong legs and tail help it propel its body through the water.

These mammals do not use their powerful legs only for swimming. They also rely on them to climb and run on land. While onshore, river otters have been known to reach speeds of up to 29 miles (47 km) per hour. Otters depend on their muscular tail for balance, as well as to defend themselves and steer while swimming.

An otter's large lungs allow it to remain underwater for as long as eight minutes at a time. Otters keep water out of their nose and ears by simply squeezing them shut when they swim.

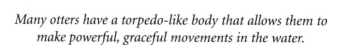

*Many otters have a torpedo-like body that allows them to make powerful, graceful movements in the water.*

# Mouth and Muzzle

An otter's mouth features 34 to 36 teeth that are adapted to its carnivorous diet. Otters have two pairs of canines. They rely on these powerful, pointed teeth to grab and bite prey and to pry open tough outer shells of certain prey. Meanwhile, an otter's premolars and molars—which are wide, flat, grinding teeth—help it crush up urchins and other hard-bodied prey.

Otters depend heavily on their nose and whiskers, too. Scientists believe that otters have a sharp sense of smell. Their whiskers, or vibrissae, are extremely sensitive as well. While an otter is swimming, these long hairs detect vibrations in the water. Together, these traits allow otters to recognize when prey, predators, and other otters are near. The vibrissae are also used to search for food in rocky, muddy areas and other hard-to-reach locations.

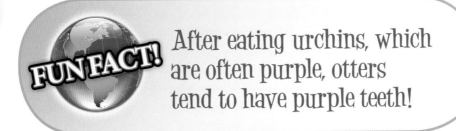

**FUN FACT!** After eating urchins, which are often purple, otters tend to have purple teeth!

*An otter frequently uses its pointed canines to grip and rip apart prey.*

# Ears, Eyes, and Intelligence

Otters have good hearing. They rely heavily on their ears to detect danger on land. Otters also have excellent vision that allows them to see both above and below the surface of the water. They are able to do this because their eyeballs are specially adapted to deal with refraction. Refraction is the process of light changing direction when it passes through water, glass, or other materials. For some animals, refraction makes it harder to view objects underwater. This is not the case for otters.

In addition to having sharp senses, otters are often considered to be among the most intelligent mammals on Earth. Scientists have observed them making tools out of rocks, wood, and empty shells. Otters are one of the few animals to possess this ability. They mainly use the simple devices they create to reach the meat of hard-bodied prey such as clams and snails.

*Otters break open clam shells by pounding them against rocks.*

# CHAPTER 3

# An Aquatic Lifestyle

Most otter species live for 10 to 20 years in the wild. This life span is generally longer in captivity, where otters face fewer threats.

Different otter species have slightly different lifestyles. For example, Eurasian and neotropical otters are typically solitary animals. They prefer to spend most of their time alone. On the other hand, sea otters and spotted-necked otters can be very social. They belong to groups called bevies, families, lodges, rafts, or romps. These groups range in size from just a few members to many otters.

In most cases, females and their pups—which are also known as kits or whelps—live in separate areas from adult males. It is not uncommon for males to become territorial, or protective of their space. This is especially true when they begin seeking out mates.

*The spotted-necked otter is named for the small patches of white fur on its neck.*

# Otter Interaction

Otters use a wide variety of noises to communicate with one another. Some of these sounds include chirping, clicking, growling, whistling, chuckling, and screaming. The exact noises otters make are often different for each species.

Scientists still have much to learn about what all these sounds mean. Otters likely use these sounds to share messages about which otters are in charge within a raft. Such noises also probably serve as warnings when otters sense danger nearby.

Otters use far more than just sounds to interact. For example, people have observed them playing games that involve wrestling, sliding, and chasing. In addition, mothers display both disapproval and affection by the ways they position their bodies and touch their pups. Otters also claim ownership of territory by marking it with their waste. Freshwater species send a similar signal using strong odors created by scent glands at the base of their tail.

*Grooming is one way that mother otters often show affection for their babies.*

# Mating Season

Otters are ready to **reproduce** when they are between two and three years old. Mating season varies among different species and different parts of the world. Otters do not usually mate for life.

The length of **gestation** varies among different species. For instance, river otters are pregnant for roughly two months. Meanwhile, scientists have determined that spotted-necked otters often don't give birth until up to 10 months after mating.

In most cases, female otters reproduce just once or twice a year. Each time, they have one to six pups. Otters that spend most of their lives in freshwater environments typically give birth on land. They have their babies in a den. For sea otters, birth takes place in the water. Instead of in a den, pups are frequently born on a bed of kelp.

*A baby otter rides on its mother's stomach as she floats on her back.*

# Growing Pups

Freshwater otter pups and sea otter pups tend to look different from each other at birth. Freshwater otter babies are born blind and without any teeth. Sea otter pups, on the other hand, enter the world with their eyes open. Their teeth are usually beginning to show as well.

At first, all newborn otters depend on their mother for food and protection. Many pups remain in the den until they are at least a few months old. Sea otters rest on their mother's stomach as she floats in the water on her back. Like most mammals, female otters produce milk to feed their young. Depending on the species, pups **nurse** for anywhere from 14 weeks to eight months.

Eventually, otter babies start to explore their surroundings. They gradually become better swimmers and learn how to catch their own food. By the time they are 6 to 12 months old, most pups are able to survive without their mother's care.

*Otter pups often play and wrestle with each other.*

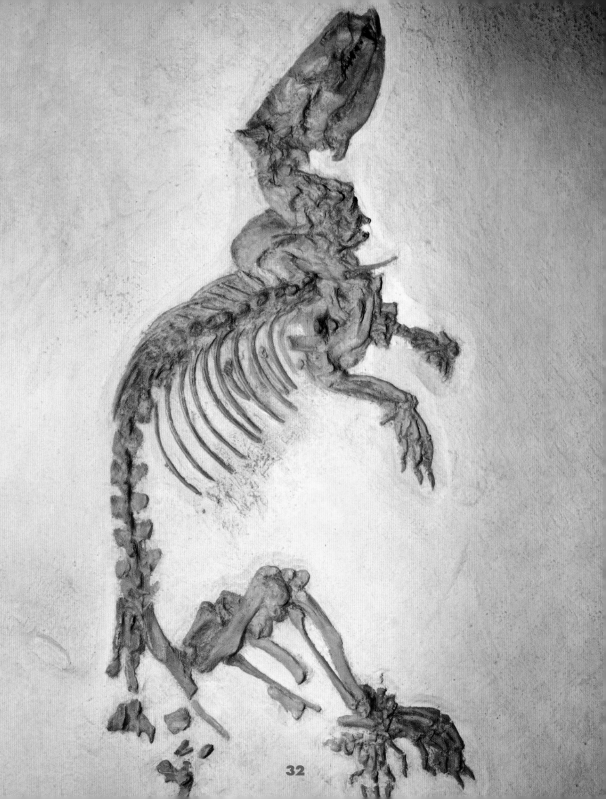

# CHAPTER 4

# The Extended Family

Scientists believe that otters' earliest ancestors first appeared about 23 million years ago. However, it was likely another 16 million to 18 million years before animals that more closely resemble modern otters appeared. At first, these creatures probably lived only on land. Eventually, they began spending more time in the water.

There are a few reasons why this may have occurred. Some experts suggest that ancient otters developed an aquatic lifestyle to avoid predators. It's also possible that the water became a more reliable source of food.

Most otters didn't completely abandon their life on land. Scientists suspect that ancient otters still returned to their dens at night even after they began hunting more in the water.

*Scientists study the fossils, or hardened remains, of early otters to learn how these animals evolved.*

# Members of Mustelidae

Otters belong to a large family of small- to medium-sized carnivorous mammals known as Mustelidae. Other members of the family include badgers, ermines, ferrets, grisons, martens, minks, polecats, tayras, weasels, and wolverines.

One of the biggest differences between otters and most other mustelids is how often they're in the water. Apart from minks, most mustelids tend to spend most of their time on land. However, all mustelids have at least a few features in common. Most have short ears and legs. In addition, each of their four feet ends in five toes. A large number of mustelids also have powerful claws and a thick coat of fur. Ermines, ferrets, grisons, martens, minks, polecats, tayras, and weasels usually have a long, slender shape. Badgers and wolverines have a broader, flatter appearance.

*Mink are among an otter's closest relatives.*

# Studying Different Species

Otters are divided into seven genera, or groups of species. These are small-clawed otters, sea otters, spotted-necked otters, American river otters, Old World river otters, smooth-coated otters, and giant otters. Differences among the genera include where they are found and how big they are. One way to tell otters apart is to study the fur on their nose. The amount and shape of the hair is different for each of the 13 species.

The name of an otter species often hints at its unique qualities. For example, the African clawless otter lacks the sharp claws that so many of its relatives have. Meanwhile, the hairy-nosed otter has short hairs on the moist, outer portion of its nose. Unfortunately, it is also one of five species of otter that are currently listed as endangered. Along with sea otters, marine otters, South American river otters, and giant otters, it faces a very high risk of becoming extinct in the wild.

*Though they lack claws, African clawless otters have rough skin on their toes to help them grip prey.*

CHAPTER 5

# What Lies Ahead

Humans and otters have a complicated relationship that stretches back hundreds of years. Part of this history involves people hunting otters. Starting in the 1700s, otter fur was used to make a wide variety of clothing, including robes for royalty.

Fishing led to a decrease in otter populations across the globe. Overfishing limited the animals' food supply. In addition, otters were often injured and killed when they became trapped in fishing nets. Sometimes people purposely harmed them to reduce competition for fish.

Human development and pollution have also taken a toll on otters. The clearing and changing of wilderness areas have damaged or destroyed many of their natural habitats. Oil spills and chemicals being dumped into the water have had a similar effect. As a result of all these activities, at least one species has been wiped off the planet. Japanese river otters were last seen in 1979. In 2012, they were officially declared extinct.

*Otters are still hunted in certain parts of the world.*

# Hope for the Future

Sadly, people continue to harm otters, both through hunting and other destructive behavior. However, **conservationists** have taken steps to save these magnificent mammals. They have worked with lawmakers to restrict the killing of otters. Conservationists also try to clean up habitats that have been affected by pollution.

Just as importantly, conservationists provide information to the public in settings ranging from classrooms to nature centers. They spend time with everyone from students to government officials to discuss the importance of sparing otters from extinction. At this point, it's impossible to know for certain if they will be successful. Nevertheless, education increases public awareness and appreciation of otters. Hopefully, people will recognize how remarkable these playful, intelligent mammals truly are. Like so many of nature's children, otters are amazing animals that deserve humans' protection and respect.

*A wildlife official in Mississippi feeds a baby otter that was abandoned by its mother.*

# Words to Know

adaptations (ah-dap-TAY-shuhnz) — changes living things go through so they fit in better with their environment

aquatic (uh-KWAH-tik) — living or growing in water

carnivorous (kahr-NIV-ur-uhs) — having meat as a regular part of the diet

conservationists (kon-sur-VAY-shun-ists) — people who work to protect an environment and the living things in it

dens (DENZ) — the homes of wild animals

environments (en-VYE-ruhn-muhnts) — the natural surroundings of living things, such as the air, land, or sea

extinct (ik-STINGKT) — no longer found alive; known about only through fossils or history

family (FAM-uh-lee) — a group of living things that are related to each other

gestation (jes-TAY-shun) — the period of time that unborn young are within the mother

glands (GLANDZ) — organs in the body that produce or release natural chemicals

grooming (GROO-ming) — cleaning and caring for hair and other physical features

habitats (HAB-uh-tats) — the places where an animal or a plant is usually found

home range (HOME RAYNJ) — area of land in which an animal spends most of its time insulates (IN-suh-layts) — prevents heat from escaping

kelp (KELP) — large, edible, brown seaweed

mammals (MAM-uhlz) — warm-blooded animals that have hair or fur and usually give birth to live babies; female mammals produce milk to feed their young

mates (MAYTS) — animals that join together to reproduce

metabolism (muh-TAB-uh-liz-uhm) — the rate at which nutrients and energy are used to maintain body functions

muzzle (MUHZ-uhl) — an animal's nose and mouth

neotropical (nee-oh-TRAH-pi-kuhl) — relating to the tropical region in Central and South America, southern Mexico, and the Caribbean

nurse (NURS) — to feed a baby milk produced by its mother

predators (PREH-duh-turz) — animals that live by hunting other animals for food

prey (PRAY) — an animal that's hunted by another animal for food

reproduce (ree-pruh-DOOS) — to produce offspring or individuals of the same kind

rodents (ROH-duhnts) — mammals with large, sharp front teeth that are constantly growing and used for gnawing things

species (SPEE-sheez) — one of the groups into which animals and plants of the same genus are divided; members of the same species can mate and have offspring

# Habitat Map

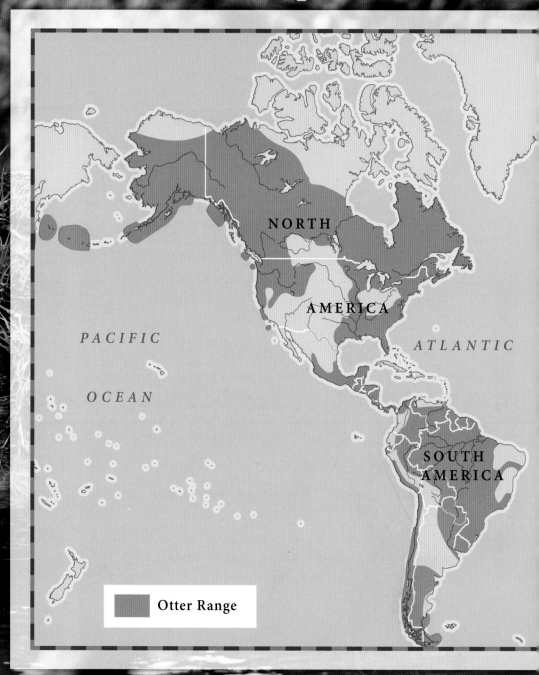

PACIFIC

OCEAN

NORTH

AMERICA

ATLANTIC

SOUTH
AMERICA

Otter Range

ARCTIC OCEAN

EUROPE

ASIA

AFRICA

PACIFIC OCEAN

OCEAN

INDIAN

OCEAN

AUSTRALIA

# Find Out More

**Books**

Gates, Margo. *Sea Otters*. Minneapolis: Bellwether Media, 2014.

Lynette, Rachel. *Giant River Otters*. New York: Bearport Publishing, 2013.

Mineo, Ella. *Sea Otters in Danger*. New York: Gareth Stevens Publishing, 2014.

Visit this Scholastic Web site for more information on otters:
**www.factsfornow.scholastic.com**
Enter the keyword **Otters**

# Index

Page numbers in *italics* indicate a photograph or map.

# About the Author

Katie Marsico is the author of more than 150 children's books. She has always loved watching otters at the aquarium and zoo. While writing this book, she enjoyed learning about the unique traits of each individual species.